POST-TRUTH?

Currents in Reformational Thought Series

Currents in Reformational Thought seeks to promote new scholarship emerging from the rich and dynamic tradition of reformational intellectual inquiry. Believing that all scholarly endeavour is rooted in and oriented by deep spiritual commitments of one kind or other, reformational scholarship seeks to add its unique Christian voice to discussions about leading questions of life and society. From this source, it seeks to contribute to the redemptive transformation and renewal of the various aspects of contemporary society, developing currents of thought that open human imagination to alternative future possibilities that may helpfully address the damage we find in present reality. As part of this work, *Currents in Reformational Thought* will bring to light the inter- and multi-disciplinary dimensions of this intellectual tradition, and promote reformational scholarship that intentionally invites dialogue with other traditions or streams of thought.

ICS | CPRSE
Institute for | Centre for Philosophy,
Christian Studies | Religion & Social Ethics

www.icscanada.edu/cprse

Robert Sweetman and Ronald A. Kuipers
SERIES EDITORS

POST-TRUTH?

FACTS AND FAITHFULNESS

Jeffrey Dudiak

Foreword by Ronald A. Kuipers
and Robert Sweetman

WIPF & STOCK · Eugene, Oregon

POST-TRUTH?
Facts and Faithfulness

Currents in Reformational Thought Series

Wipf & Stock
An Imprint of Wipf and Stock Publishers
199 W. 8th Ave., Suite 3
Eugene, OR 97401

www.wipfandstock.com

PAPERBACK ISBN: 978-1-6667-0646-8
HARDCOVER ISBN: 978-1-6667-0647-5
EBOOK ISBN: 978-1-6667-0648-2

02/24/22

CONTENTS

CONTENTS

FOREWORD

THE SLIM BOOK YOU are now holding is as timely as it is important, and its deep wisdom will ensure that it remains important even when it becomes less timely. Do not let its small size fool you. In these brief pages Jeffrey Dudiak eloquently explores the fissures and fractures that vex our so-called 'post-truth' era, searching for a deeper, dare we say truer, understanding of the cultural forces that have led North American society to become so polarized. How should we understand the fact that so many people today—progressive or conservative, left or right—gravitate toward mutually exclusive versions of the truth, and in so doing turn a blind eye to or explain away any facts that might trouble their increasingly strident ideological take on the world? Has the entire Christian world itself been sucked into this vortex, or does this spiritual lifeway still harbour resources to help us approach such fractious polarization with a healing word, a bridge toward social solidarity, justice, peace, and right relations with our fellow human and non-human creatures?

If you have come to this book with questions like these, we confidently venture to say that you will not leave it disappointed. While these are not easy questions to answer, Dudiak is able to approach them with wit, wisdom, and a wonderfully wry sense of humour. Eschewing the kind of easy answers that trade pluralistic solidarity for tribalistic certainty, Dudiak diagnoses a deeper breakdown in social trust as the underlying issue that has everyone today scurrying for comforting, ideological cover. In this context,

Dudiak reminds the reader that truth is more, and runs deeper, than simple correspondence to the facts.

The faithfulness we owe to facts, Dudiak argues, is but one aspect of a deeper understanding of truth as *faithfulness*, and on this understanding there are more things we need to be faithful to than just facts. There is even a sense, Dudiak says, in which the totality of verified facts that characterizes our damaged present, or *what is now the case*, is false. For example, those who strive to follow the Christian lifeway, if they are truly listening, heed a call to keep faith with the vision that scripture offers of a redeemed and restored future in which justice and peace embrace. Such a Christian, then, must come to terms with the idea that *what is not (yet)* might be, in an important moral and ethical sense, truer than *what is*.

Given Dudiak's deft handling of these weighty questions, this book makes a fitting and powerful contribution to the *Currents in Reformational Thought* book series sponsored by the Institute for Christian Studies. This series seeks to publish Christian scholarship that is interdisciplinary in its implications, philosophically primed in its conceptual strategies, theologically literate, and spiritually aware in its depth orientation. Possessing all these virtues, the book more than meets the series' goal of making a scholarly contribution to human flourishing in relation to ordinary human experience and understanding of the world—as a servant of that experience and understanding rather than as a detached arbiter of it. As a result, it exudes a deep spiritual awareness of the interplay of sin and Grace throughout the creation we inhabit, a creation made for the flourishing of its creatures in communion with its Creator. Dudiak's book takes full advantage, then, of the series' desire to create a space where authors may fully own their orienting spiritual impulse, their *faithfulness*, while remaining open to the presence of wisdom wherever it is to be found. For these reasons and more, we are extremely pleased to welcome *Post-Truth? Facts and Faithfulness* as the third volume of this series.

Ronald A. Kuipers and Robert Sweetman
Toronto, June 2021

ACKNOWLEDGMENTS

In an age when we are not only questioning *what is true*, but in which *truth itself* is under assault, it is perhaps especially incumbent upon Christians—followers of Jesus, who claimed to be "the way, the truth, and the life"—to reflect deeply upon the kind of truth to which we aspire. The argument of this little book is that *"the current crisis in truth is the effect of an impoverished sense of truth*. That is, what we understand by truth today is too narrow, too emaciated, too weak, and too fragile to support the weight that we of necessity place upon truth, and it is crumbling under the load. *We need therefore, a richer sense of truth, one that is thicker, more profound, more robust.* I am going to argue that this richer sense of truth is already part of our religio-cultural heritage, so is still available to us, but that we have largely lost sight of it, because it has been eclipsed by the prevailing, impoverished sense. I want to explore how we can recover this richer sense of truth" (quoted from Chapter One of this book).

The three short chapters that follow are a slightly edited version of the three lectures that I gave at the Interdisciplinary Studies conference at The King's University, Edmonton, on September 19th and 20th, 2018, on the theme of "Post-Truth." While I have made some minor changes to the script to accommodate the transition to print, and to make it more accessible to an audience that was not on-site and thus privy to internal references, I have tried to retain the conversational style that I hope will make this book welcoming to an intelligent, but not necessarily academic, audience. And while some of the cultural references may have passed their "expiry date" by the time of publication, I trust that the points they are employed to illustrate endure. These lectures were first published as a short book by The King's University Press in 2019, for largely "in-house" use, for distribution among supporters, alumni, and students of the University. When my good friend Ronald Kuipers, president of the Institute for Christian Studies, suggested to me the possibility of re-issuing the book in the *Currents in Reformational Thought* series, I was grateful for the prospect of broader distribution than the first publication afforded, and my colleagues at King's were more than pleased to see this material reappear in a book series sponsored by one of our "sister" institutions.

Indeed, such a move seemed to me highly appropriate. As a graduate of the Institute for Christian Studies (ICS) myself, I am grateful for the many ways in which the Reformationally-oriented approaches to life and thought taught at ICS have left an indelible mark upon my understanding of myself and the world in which I live. My hope is that my immersion in this approach as a graduate student, stirred together with the Quaker sensibilities that have been inculcated in me across a lifetime of involvement with that religious society, have allowed me to produce a text that will invite a broad range of others to consider again their own approaches to truth, and its relationship to Christian faithfulness.

So, my thanks to Ronald Kuipers, and his colleague Robert Sweetman, for the opportunity to publish in the *Currents in Reformational Thought* series that ICS sponsors through Wipf and Stock, and to my friends Nik Ansell and Gideon Strauss, also of ICS, who were early in bringing attention to the text among ICS readers. Deep gratitude also to Héctor Acero Ferrer for his diligent work in editing and formatting the text for this publication.

I reiterate my thanks to those at The Kings University in Edmonton who invited me to give the Interdisciplinary Studies Lectures, and proceed toward publication, especially Rebecca Warren, Dr. Hank Bestman, and Dr. Arlette Zinck, and the IS Faculty Committee for the year 2017–18 (Lloyd den Boer, Neal

DeRoo, Amy Feaver, Randy Haluza-Delay, Doug Harink, and Tim Wood) and the IS Student Committee for the same year (Megan Apperloo, Derrick Adams, Ashley Barrett-Hamilton, Grace Bigazi, Anna Boessenkool, Sara Himer, Brody Hite, Izzy Jones, Caleb Koning, Karen Lietz, Amanda Nsofor, Mark Unruh, and Henri van den Berg).

At The King's University we are committed to student engaged research, so it was a pleasure for me to invite the students in two of my courses to work through the lectures with me, and to make comments, many of which were very insightful. The first was my Epistemology course in the fall of 2018, consisting of Rachel Boone, Conrad Bremont, Lama Chammas, Ciara Fraser, Brady Gamroth, Bailey Giesbrecht, Kyle Gooler, Janessa Gritter, Jaybyn Gross, Abigail Hartung, Liam Hofstede, Kenneth Jackson, Lydin Johnson, Deanna Kool, Pablo Montano, Nina Munsey, Holly Parker, Cameron Schlamp, Elizabeth Shapko, McKenzie Tilstra, Janki Trivedi, Sydney Warchola, and Meesha Wittkoff. Among other things, these students helped me to think more deeply about how (and whether) to make a case for an alternative sense of truth in a time when the predominant sense is so overwhelmingly powerful that it is hard to think of truth in any other way, and helped me better guard against the impression that I am speaking against science when I am simply hoping to delimit it in a way that is faithful to the scientific project itself.

The second course in which students were invited to interact with the material of the lectures was the Senior Philosophy Seminar in the winter of 2019. Students in this class—consisting of Anna Boesenkool, Edison Cardinal, Brian Lardner, Katie MacCrimmon, Dempsey Strand, Theoren Tolsma, and Mark Unruh—engaged the lectures in the pursuit of their own reflections on truth in relation to some of their own concerns. I was inspired and challenged by their work. Special thanks go to Katie MacCrimmon, then a graduating English major and Philosophy minor, who went carefully through the manuscript and provided a number of helpful editorial suggestions. I did not always take her advice, as I wanted to preserve something of my idiosyncratic voice and phrasing, but often I did.

So, what of truth, and particularly Christian truth, in our post-truth era? I warmly invite you, the reader, to engage with me on this contentious issue. So perplexing. So crucial.

Jeffrey Dudiak
Edmonton, August 2020

CHAPTER 1

POST-TRUTH: FACTS AND FAITHFULNESS

1. The post-truth era

BACK IN 2005, WHEN people still used to watch TV, before everybody under thirty simply ignored cable and started watching YouTube instead, Stephen Colbert, the comedian who is currently the host of "The Late Show" on CBS, had a television program on Comedy Central called "The Colbert Report" in which he played the role of a conservative talk-show host, confusingly named Stephen Colbert, in which he nightly mocked advocates of right-wing politics by pretending to be one of them, their foibles and blind-spots coming vividly to life across Colbert's hilarious parody. One of Colbert's recurring bits was to accuse—by pretending to advocate for—the presidential administration of the time, that of George W. Bush, and conservatives in general, of relying not upon the truth, but rather upon something Colbert called "truthiness." According to Colbert, with regard to truthiness: "We're not talking about the truth; we're talking about something that seems like truth—the truth we want to exist."[1] And Wikipedia defines truthiness (its word of the year in 2005) as "a truth 'known' intuitively by the user without regard to evidence, logic, intellectual examination or facts." The "character" Stephen Colbert—as opposed to the actor Stephen Colbert, who played the character Stephen

---

1. https://en.wikipedia.org/wiki/Truthiness. Accessed 8 April, 2019.

Colbert—would often mockingly advocate for some inane political position on the show—say, for instance, the Bush administration's denial of climate change—by appealing to what his "gut" told him, over against what all of the reasoned evidence suggests.[2]

But "truthiness" has affected not only the political right. Rather, we are told that we live in a post-truth era. Lagging a full decade behind Colbert's keen, if comically framed, identification of this qualifying characteristic of our *Zeitgeist* (the spirit of our times), and in "honour" of the political climate exemplified and ratcheted up by the Trump administration, "post-truth" was named the *Oxford Dictionaries'* "international word of the year" in 2016.[3] It is there defined as: "Relating to or denoting circumstances in which objective facts are less influential in shaping public opinion than appeals to emotion and personal belief."

The word "post" here means "after," in the sense that "post-traumatic stress disorder" is something that one suffers "after" some traumatic event. We are also told that we live in a "post-Christian era." That means that we live after the time when Christianity, at least in our western culture, could be assumed to have appeal for everyone (or at least almost everyone). A couple of generations ago one could still appeal to the Bible to make a point about some or other matter of public policy, and that would carry weight; anymore, such an appeal no longer has traction with a sufficient number of people to be effective. That is what it means to live in a post-Christian society. It is not that no one is a Christian anymore; it is not even that

---

2. To see this played out to its bizarre but hilarious extreme, see Colbert's address at the 2006 White House Correspondents' Association dinner, broadly available on YouTube.

3. "Post-truth seems to have been first used in this meaning in a 1992 essay by the late Serbian-American playwright Steve Tesich in *The Nation* magazine. Reflecting on the Iran-Contra scandal and the Persian Gulf War, Tesich lamented that 'we, as a free people, have freely decided that we want to live in some post-truth world'. There is evidence of the phrase 'post-truth' being used before Tesich's article, but apparently with the transparent meaning 'after the truth was known', and not with the new implication that truth itself has become irrelevant. A book, *The Post-truth Era*, by Ralph Keyes appeared in 2004, . . . " https://en.oxforddictionaries.com/word-of-the-year/word-of-the-year-2016. Accessed 1 September, 2018.

the majority of the population are no longer Christian; rather, it is that Christianity can no longer be assumed as a sufficiently broad, shared point of appeal that it can be relied upon as a touchstone for adjudicating political controversies. Similarly, we are told that we live in a post-modern era, meaning that the shared assumptions of the historical period referred to as modernism can no longer be relied upon to attract general consensus. About that I will have more to say in the next chapter.

For now, let us focus on what it means to live in a post-truth world, that is, in our world, the one that you and I, according to this observation, inhabit today, a world in which *we* (as a society) really do not believe in truth anymore. That does not mean that no one believes in truth anymore, but that there are no longer any authorities who are capable of providing us with truth claims that are acknowledged to be true by a broad general consensus, truths upon which we all basically agree. That state of affairs affects everyone, whether we agree with it or not, whether we like it or not. It affects me, and it affects you.

Consider the following questions. When a politician tells you something, do you believe that it is true? I suspect that most of you are pretty suspicious of what politicians say. Why? Because you know that a lot of the time a politician is going to say what they need to say in order to get elected, or re-elected, rather than because it is true. Okay, but what about your pastors? When your pastor tells you something, do you automatically believe that it is true? Many of you have grown up in contexts where you were not really allowed to question religious authority, because to do so was to risk your salvation, but many of you do anyway. Why? Because your pastor has a point of view that is not necessarily your own. You have your own life, and experiences, and ideas. Further, when your parents tell you something, do you necessarily believe that it is true? Your parents grew up in a different era, way back when phones were plugged into a wall, when pot was illegal, and they do not even know the difference between Drake and Kanye, so how could what they say be true to your reality? Or, as another of my favourite comedians, Woody Allen, has one of his characters say:

"Everything our parents said was good is bad: sun, milk, red meat, . . . college."[4] And, while we are on the subject of college, what about your professors? Do you believe that what they say is true just because they say so? I certainly do not, and I am one. Even the claims of science, *the* authority with respect to what is true for the past two or three centuries (a subject to which I will return in more detail in chapter two), are in question in our age. Whether or not there is human-induced global warming is in genuine question in very many quarters, despite what over 97 percent of climate scientists are saying.[5] Moreover, do not scientists keep changing their minds, anyway? I remember as a kid being scared out of my wits because scientists were predicting the oncoming of another ice age, and I laid in bed at night designing in my mind something like a huge electric hair dryer with which I planned to save my neighbourhood from the encroaching threat. Now I have to lie in bed at night and imagine employing a giant ice cube! And even if you do trust in scientific authorities, what happens when they contradict each other, as they very often do?

So, the question is, whom do you believe? Or, whom do you not believe? Why? On what authority? And why trust that authority? Truth is confusing, at best. Some of us believe that there is a truth, but that it is hard if not impossible to find, because truth is always being manipulated by those with the power to make us believe that something is true when it is really just in their best interest to make us believe that it is true. This is a position called *cynicism*, which asserts that there is a truth, but I am always suspicious of anybody's claim that what they say is the truth, because everybody is always spinning the truth, and I am always afraid that I am being played. Others of us believe that while there may be a truth, it is impossible for us, for us human beings with our finite perspectives and our limited brain capacity, to discover it, at least in any way that would be full enough to constitute "the truth." This position, that it is in principle impossible to know the truth, is

4. Allen, *Annie Hall.* Accessed October 27, 2021.

5. According to my colleague and astrophysicist, Professor emeritus Brian Martin.

called *skepticism*. And once we admit that no one has certain access to *the* truth, we get *relativism*, the idea that there really is no truth that is true for everybody at all; rather, the truth is always relative to, that is, it depends upon, the position and preferences of the one claiming such truth. Muslims have their truth and Christians have a different truth. What is true for you is not necessarily true for me; every group, even every individual, has their own perspective, so has their own truth. So whether I am suspicious of those who claim to provide me with the truth (as in cynicism), or suspicious of our human capacities to really know the truth (as in skepticism), or suspicious of the very idea of objective truth itself, that is, that there is a truth that is true for everybody (as in relativism), ours is a time when we are, in light of all of the confusion and ambiguity, at least tempted to trust our guts, our intuitions, our emotions, and personal preferences, rather than any outside authority's attempts to provide us with the truth. Given all of these complications, all of this confusion around truth, is not my truth as valid as any other, at least for me? And even if we do, as individuals or small groups, trust certain authorities to supply us with reliable truths, we no longer *as a culture* share trust in the same authorities—and that lack of shared trust causes many to question the viability of truth altogether. That is what it means to live in a post-truth age. So if you have some serious suspicions, or at least reservations, about truth, you should not be surprised. That is what it means to be part of our post-truth culture today. That is our reality.

2. Truth matters

So we all inhabit, and our young people are coming of age in, a time when there is every reason to have doubts about the truth, to suspect that we cannot really know the truth, that what we are told is the truth is just some form of manipulation, or that the truth is really just a name for what we happen to believe here and now. That is our cultural mood, and if students today are some-times under-prepared in terms of certain academic fundamentals, they are all products of over-exposure to media and are all keenly attuned to our cultural environment. For this reason, if you are still in the first three or four decades of life, you, more than any generation before you, are worldly-wise, street-smart, and you have imbibed the cultural suspicion about the truth as if through your pores. Many of you suffer under your doubts about the truth, almost afraid to admit them, while others of you embrace these doubts and wear them like a badge of sophistication and courage, revelling in your nouveau existentialist chic. Or you have decided that it is all too much for you, and you focus on what you can control, like binge-watching "The Office" or "Breaking Bad." But as products of your times, you cannot but have your doubts. And I want to assure you that that is not entirely a bad thing (although you may not believe that I am telling you the truth either!). There is a good reason why you have your doubts. The rest of us do, too. I hope to explain to you later why I think that is.

But before we get to that, I want to suggest to you that even though you will have your doubts about truth, and regardless of all of your doubts, the truth matters to you, and it matters a lot.

So, by way of example, let us imagine that you have decided to attend university. Why? Because somebody told you that being at university will improve your prospects for a better life, and you believed them. In fact, you are investing a lot of your life to attend university, betting that the promise that university will make your life better is true. You are investing a good deal of money in order to go, and chances are that in order to afford it you will be working jobs that make being at school more challenging, and taking out loans that you will one day have to repay. Perhaps you are blessed that a parent or grandparent is helping you with the costs, but that is not free either, because it is money you will not be getting in your inheritance later. Or you have scholarships or grants and somebody else is making this investment on your behalf. But it is not only the money. Being a university student requires a huge investment of your time and energy. You need to study, write papers, complete assignments, prepare for exams, and do all of that under the pressure of time and the expectations of your family and your professors and yourself. There will be times when things will just not be working out, when you will be frustrated with what you do not understand and just do not seem to be able to get your thick head around, and you will throw your book across your dorm room, tear out your hair, scream some obscenity, and want to quit. But you will see it though (I hope). Being at university takes a lot out of you, requires of you an investment of blood, sweat, and tears, not to mention dollars, dollars you are spending being at school instead of dollars you could be making by going out and getting a job. You pay a significant price in any number of ways to be at university, risking a lot, all based upon a promise: that your life will be "richer" (and not only monetarily) if you attend university than it will be if you do not. But what if that is not true? What if you put in your four hard years and just end up selling raffle tickets at the bowling alley anyway? What if the whole thing is just an elaborate ruse set up by the professors to enrich themselves by charging you exorbitant tuition fees for a bunch of useless classes that are only going to set you back in life? Then you will have been duped, cheated, made a fool of, and I bet you would be pretty angry about that. The truth matters, and it matters to you.

Your doctor tells you that the drug he or she is prescribing for you will help to clear up your skin, rather than make it worse. And it had better, because otherwise you will end up like the author of this book and go through four years of university without getting a date, and nobody wants that. The truth matters, and it matters to you.

Or let us imagine that you, over the next few years, hope to be standing before an altar with your beloved, and that person is going to tell you that he or she is going to be faithful to you "till death do you part." You are going to invest all that you have in that person, every aspect of your life: emotional, sexual, financial, and spiritual. This person will be your closest relationship, the heart of your heart and the hearth of your home. And if it turns out that that person cannot keep the vow on the basis of which you have invested in them everything you are and have, if (for whatever reason) they break their promise, it is going to break you: emotionally, sexually, financially, and spiritually. The scriptures speak of husband and wife becoming one flesh, and that God frowns on divorce; this is not, however (as is sometimes implied), because God has some kind of obsession with moral purity, but because God loves us, and no one should have to suffer the tearing of their flesh because the promise that was once made turns out to have been a lie (however sincere your partner was in making it at the time). The truth matters, and it matters to you.

Not to mention all of the ways in which "we" need the truth, collectively, in order to negotiate the difficult challenges of climate and economics and health and politics and justice and peace. It matters whether or not our industrial practices are precipitating climate change or not. It matters whether cutting taxes benefits or further cripples the poor. It matters whether a policy of peace through strength really leads to stability or just masks a more subtle form of war. The truth matters, it matters a lot, and it matters to us all.

So you—young people in particular, but the rest of you too—are in a very awkward position. The truth matters profoundly to you, and, yet, you live in an historical time that is characterized as being a post-truth age. As members of your culture, you are not quite sure you believe in truth, and yet, your life, or at least if your life is to have quality, depends upon it.

In this little book, I want to try and make some sense of this troubling situation, to consider whether there might not be a way that we can think about truth (and experience the truth, indeed, to be in the truth) that would take us beyond the current crisis of truth into a healthier and more redemptive relationship to it. That is, I will advocate here for truth as essential to our lives, while taking fully seriously the objections to truth that have precipitated the post-truth era. It cannot be a matter of just closing our eyes, clicking our heels, and hoping we will find ourselves home safely in the land of untroubled truth. Our contemporary suspicions about "the truth" are well-founded, and need to be honoured, even if—I will suggest—we need not get stuck in them. To put things crudely, I want to ask the questions: "What went wrong with truth?" and "How do we fix it?"

Now, because we have limited time, I am going to spill the beans. I am going to jump to the conclusion and tell you how the story I am going to tell is going to come out, and then I will go back and try to give an account of how we got there. My central thesis in this chapter, which will form the focus of everything else I am going to say, is this: *the current crisis in truth is the effect of an impoverished sense of truth*. That is, what we understand by truth today is too narrow, too emaciated, too weak, and too fragile to support the weight that we of necessity place upon truth, and it is crumbling under the load. *We need, therefore, a richer sense of truth, one that is thicker, more profound, and more robust*. I am going to argue that this richer sense of truth is already part of our religio-cultural heritage, so is still available to us, but that we have largely lost sight of it because it has been eclipsed by the currently prevailing, impoverished sense of truth. I want to explore how we can recover this richer sense of truth.

3. The truth today

Students who have had me for class know that one of my fantasies (one of the recurring thoughts that I entertain myself with when I have insomnia) is that I am driving my Jaguar convertible along the Pacific coast highway accompanied by the English actress Helena Bonham Carter. The salty mist from the thudding surf is blowing through my hair as I carve a sweeping curve with the Jag, a startling vista of rocky cliffs and shimmering beach coming into view before us. Helena looks at me adoringly, reaching over to caress the back of my neck, as we sing along to The Beatles' "Love me do" on the radio. It is shallow of me, I know, but it is a good fantasy; it has gotten me through many a sleepless night. But it is just a *fantasy*; it is not *true*. While I may entertain *the idea* that I have a Jaguar convertible in my garage, *the fact* is that I drive a 2012 Volkswagen Passat, which is nice enough, but it is no Jaguar XKE. While I can *imagine* that I am married to Helena Bonham Carter, *the fact* is that she does not even know I am alive. (At least, she does not answer any of my letters.) My fantasy is *just a fantasy* because it is *not true*; what it conjures up in imagination is not real; it does not align with the facts. And for us, today, the measure of the truth is what is real, is the facts. What is considered true is oriented toward what is the case, or the naming of what is the case.

The truth, in this sense, is therefore distinguished from "what is not the case," which then is patently not true. What is not true, moreover, can come to the fore in a variety of ways. First, as we have been discussing, it can happen in fantasy, in imagination. When I am driving my Passat, I can (and sometimes do) pretend that it is a Jaguar, but no matter how often or how effectively I am able to imagine that I am driving a Jag, *in fact*, I am still driving a Passat. That is sad, but it is the truth. It is also possible that I can be mistaken, and I take something that is not for something that is. Maybe I slip on the ice on the way to my car, bang my head and start to hallucinate, and when I climb into my Volkswagen I see the Jaguar's brushed aluminum center console, and then I turn the key and I hear that kitten roar. I truly think I am in the Jag, but because of my concussion I am delusional; it is actually not the case that I am in an XKE. The truth is that I am still in the V-Dub. It is also possible that I intentionally depart from the truth for the purposes of misleading somebody about it, that is, that I lie. Per impossible, were I ever to meet Helena Bonham Carter, I would want to do everything I could to impress her, so that maybe, just maybe, I might have a chance. So I would at least be tempted to tell her about the midnight black, classic 1963 Jaguar convertible in mint condition that I have at home in my garage, when in fact what is in my garage is a midnight blue, standard model 2012 Passat with some scratches along the side that were put there by some poor old guy who tried unsuccessfully to parallel park along side of me, and whom I did not have the heart to pursue for financial compensation. Here I am lying (sorry Helena) because what I am saying, that I own a Jag, is not the case; if I was saying what was the case, that I am the proud owner of a Passat, I would be telling the truth. So, whether it is over against fantasy, or over against error, or over against lying, in each case *the measure of the truth is what is the case over against what is not the case*. That is what, for the most part today, in our society, we mean by the truth. (In the next chapter, I will attempt to provide you with a brief account of *why* that is the case.)

There is, however, another sense of "truth" that, while less intuitive to us, is nevertheless important to understanding truth. In fact, I will be arguing that this other sense of truth, one that is not tied to the idea of "what is the case," is essential to understanding truth, and it is to an exploration of that sense of truth that I would like now to turn.

4. Truth as faithfulness

Not *so* very long ago, in fact, even when I was a kid (half-a-century ago), when you got married to someone you would say to them, as part of the marriage vows: "I pledge you my troth." If you consider the word "troth," you will notice that it looks, and sounds, a lot like the word "truth," and that is because "troth" is the Old English word that evolved into our present day word "truth." Troth means truth.[6] So when you would say to someone on your wedding day, "I pledge you my troth," what you were saying in more modern language was "I promise you my truth," or, more idiomatically, what you are saying is: "I promise to be true to you." But what does it mean to be *true* to someone? It means to be *faithful* to someone. So when on your wedding day you pledge someone your troth, you are promising to be faithful to them. The word troth, or truth, here, *means* "faithfulness." We still occasionally use the term truth in this sense in other contexts too, like when we speak of a true friend—that is, a friend who sticks by you through thick and thin, a faithful friend rather than a false friend, one who is not only your friend when they are profiting from the friendship, but who

6. My colleague in Medieval English, Brett Roscoe, provides a lovely analysis of this etymology across a reading of John 14:6 and Chaucer's poem "Truth" in the Fall 2018 issue of *King's Connection* (The King's University news for alumni and friends), 24. Three quotations from this article: "In the Middle Ages, truth primarily meant loyalty, fidelity, and the keeping of one's word." . . . "To be faithful (true) we must learn to see the world—and ourselves in it—with holy imagination." . . . "So what is truth? Chaucer suggests it is faithful living, faithful seeing, and faithful storytelling, all of which depend on the Faithful One who created and sustains all things."

is your friend even when it costs them something. Another trace of this sense of truth still marks our language when we speak of "being true to your school"—believing in and cheering for our team even when those so-and-so's from our rival school are ten points up in the fourth quarter.

Now, this sense of truth is *not* the same sense of truth that I highlighted in the last section. Truth as faithfulness does not mean the same thing as truth as fact. They are related, of course, but they are not the same. When you say that you will be true to your spouse, part of that *is* a matter of telling them the truth. You are not being true to your spouse if you tell him or her that you are visiting a sick friend in the hospital when in fact you are out knocking back pints with your buddies. But *being true* means *more* than just *telling the truth*. If you are honest with your spouse and confess that you are having an affair, that does not make you faithful. *Truth as faithfulness* means more, and something very different, than *truth as facts*. Something else is going on here.

For when you say "I pledge you my troth," or, which is to say the same thing, "I promise to be true" or "I promise to be faithful," you are not focusing on *what is* the case, which is the standard for truth in the sense of facts, but you are oriented toward *what is not* the case. When you promise your spouse on your wedding day that you will be true to them, that you will be faithful to them, you are not naming something that is *already* the case, but something that is *not yet* the case. When you promise to be faithful until death do you part, you have not done it yet. *It is not a fact; it is a promise.* Now, if you make it through you wedding day without cheating on your new spouse—congratulations! That is a good start! But nobody is going to say that you are a faithful spouse. Not yet. And, if things go as they are supposed to, your faithfulness will not yet be a fact (an "accomplished fact," a *fait accompli*, as the French so wonderfully put it) until death does separate you from your beloved, and you have fought the good fight and been faithful every day for however long God gifts you to each other. Until then, it will always be a promise, a promise you need to wake up and make over and over again, every day. Promises do not name something that "is," some fact or other, but name precisely "what is not" the case, but what will, one day, be true, if the promise is kept, that is, if you are true to your promise. If truth as fact is oriented toward the present time, and names *what is the case*, truth as faithfulness is oriented toward the future, to *what is not the case*, but some day might be the case. Truth in the sense of faithfulness does not then, like truth in the sense of facts, identify something that "is," but in a certain sense creates something that "is not, but might be, should be, and, if you keep the faith, will be." Across your kept promise to be faithful you become faithful, but only to the degree that you keep reaffirming the promise to be true. The day you pledge your troth, if you mean it, you are already being a faithful spouse, but you are only a faithful spouse if you reaffirm the promise, tomorrow, next month, next year, and four decades from now.

The difference between truth as fact, the predominant sense of truth in our modern-day society, and truth as faithfulness, is important and significant. This is particularly the case because in the modern world, the world in which to a large extent we all find ourselves living today, what counts as the truth is what science tells us is the truth, and scientists are better than anybody at telling us what is the case. All hail to science and the amazing truths that it discovers and all of the wonderful uses to which those truths can be put! Again, I will say more about how this situation came to be in the next chapter, but because we have all but equated the idea of truth with what science tells us, and because scientists are experts in telling us what is the case, we have come to equate the truth with facts, and facts of the scientific variety in particular. Consequently, anything that is not the case, that is not factually true (i.e., in our age: scientifically verifiable), is not taken to be true at all, but either false, or mere fantasy. The sense of truth as faithfulness, truth as oriented to what is not the case, gets excluded from the idea of truth.

What I want to suggest to you in this book is that the modern eclipsing of the idea of truth as faithfulness in favor of equating the idea of truth with facts, reducing truth to facts at the expense of an idea of truth that includes the idea of faithfulness, is the impoverishment of truth that lies behind our current crisis in truth, and that therefore lies behind the post-truth era. I will argue for a richer view of truth, one in which truth as fact is not the principle or governing sense of truth, but is rather a sub-category of the richer and fuller sense of truth as faithfulness. Truth as fact is one kind of faithfulness, the faithfulness of some statement of fact to the facts themselves; but this is only one kind of faithfulness, one kind of truth. There are others.

5. Christian truth

When I speak of the modern world,[7] I mean the world in which science—modern, methodological, empirical science—is taken as the primary, sometimes even the exclusive, authority on matters of truth. In the modern age, we only *really* believe what science tells us; everything else is suspect. If in the Middle Ages you wanted to find someone to provide expert commentary on some subject for your television program you would invite someone wearing clerical robes; in the modern age, you invite someone in a lab coat. Scientists are the priests of the modern age. Science replaces, and stands over against, myths and traditions and the old authorities: medical doctors replace medicine men; psychologists replace priests; research replaces common sense; textbooks replace Holy Scriptures; knowledge replaces wisdom, and—you can see where I am going with this—truth as fact replaces truth as faithfulness.

Now, within the Christian community, wherein we aspire to understand the world through the lens of the life, death, and resurrection of Jesus Christ, something that we believe is still the

---

7. The modern world is the "world" that has been emerging over roughly the last four centuries in the Occident, and that perhaps reached its ascendency in the previous century at about the same time that it came to be challenged by what has come to be known as the "post-modern" age, namely, the age (that many trace to the traumas of the World Wars, and others trace back to certain eccentric figures of the nineteenth Century) in which the fundamental doctrines of modernity became incredulous even as its influence continued to spread. Many of the central tensions of the past century and continuing into our own can be understood as arising from the tension between these two ways of understanding, these two competing, intellectual "moods."

central truth of our lives today, we seem to be at odds with this modern emphasis on science as the sole source of reliable truth, because the truth of the gospel message cannot be proven scientifically. We ground our lives in a truth that is not a scientific truth. Even so, I want to suggest that we too—even those of us who are committed to the truth of the Christian message—have been influenced by the modern age in a way that we usually do not even notice, and that affects the very way that we understand our Christianity. For while we *as Christians* confess a truth that is not a scientific truth, *as moderns* we tend to understand that truth in a modern way: that is, we understand the truth of our Christianity on the model of truths of fact, rather than as the truth of faithfulness. That does not mean we are not faithful, but too often (at least on my view) we understand our faithfulness as faithfulness to a certain series of facts that we confess.

For example, when over twenty years ago I took up my faculty position at The King's University, a Christian, liberal arts institution, in order to be hired I had to sign a "statement of faith." On that statement of faith there were a series of doctrinal truths that I was being asked to agree to if I was going to get the job: statements about the sovereignty of God, the incarnation, the trinity, the Bible, all pretty standard, orthodox Christian doctrines that obviously, since I took the position, I was able to say with sincerity that I believed. Yet, being asked to do that felt strange to me—not because I did not agree with what I was being asked to affirm (I did), but because it did not feel deep enough to me. I did not say anything at the time, because I wanted the job and did not want to be contrary, but I felt like saying: "If you want to know if I am faithful, do not ask me to sign some paper saying what I believe, but follow me around for a month. See how I behave when I am confronted by a homeless person. Watch what I do when my son is driving me crazy, yet again. Take a look at my bank statement and see where my heart really is." That is, do not ask for my statement of faith, but ask if I am faithful. Do not ask me what facts I believe to be true, ask whether or not I live truly, that is, faithfully. Now, to be clear, it is not that what we believe to be the case is unimportant; it is important!—and so I do not blame The King's University for asking those of us on faculty to sign a statement of faith. (Besides, following prospective faculty members around for a month would be pretty creepy!) But remember that the truth of facts is only one kind of truth, a subcategory of a much richer truth: truth as faithfulness. Truths of fact, I am arguing, are expressions of a deeper truth, the truth of faithfulness; our faithfulness does not answer to truths of fact. (I will have to develop that thought further in chapter three.)

For now, let me suggest to you that when the Bible speaks of truth, it is not primarily concerned with truths of fact, but with truth as faithfulness. It is not that the Bible does not contain facts, but those facts are in the service of expressing and encouraging faithfulness, which provides them with the meaning that they have; on their own, as mere facts, they are insignificant. That there was, roughly five millennia ago, a bush burning in the dessert but not being consumed may be a curious event considered on its own, but we affirm it not as a mere fact, but as an expression of God's covenant faithfulness to his people. A first century, Palestinian Jew turning water into wine might, on its own, be something that would impress even David Blaine, but we affirm it not as a magic trick, but as an expression of Jesus's gift to us of abundant life. Even the resurrection, startling if considered as a stand-alone historical fact, is only really significant to us because we are permitted to be participants in this resurrection, in this expression of the victory of life over death. The Bible contains truths of fact, but the truth with which it is occupied, that it is concerned to express and teach, is the truth of faithfulness.

One of the key indications of this is that Jesus is perpetually turning our attention to what he refers to as the Kingdom of God, or the Kingdom of Heaven. Now, the Kingdom of God is presented by Jesus in contrast to the kingdoms of this world. Over against "what is," over against the reality of war and oppression and poverty and illness and slavery, Jesus invites us into a vision of the way that the world "should be, but is not." The world should be the Kingdom of God, but rather is dominated by what Paul calls "powers and principalities" that operate contrary to the will of God. Over against "what is the case," Jesus focusses on "what is not the case," and calls us to participate with him, not in acquiescing in the facts, but in imagining what the world could be, should be, and, we trust, one day will be. Indeed, the Apostle Paul, in 1 Corinthians 1:28, tells us that God uses *the things that are not*, a literal translation of the Greek *ta me onta*, to confound *the things that are*.

Moreover, the truth of the Kingdom, what is not, is for Jesus and his followers *more true* than the truth of facts. The *fact* is that we live in a world that is at war; the *truth* is that we are called to peace. The *fact* is that the world is filled with inequality and oppression; the *truth* is love and forgiveness. The *fact* is that we are hopelessly divided against each other; the *truth* is that in the Kingdom there is neither male nor female, Greek nor Jew, conservative nor liberal. In the Kingdom discourses of Jesus and his followers "what is not" is the judge of "what is"; the truth is not measured by "what is" the case, but by "what is not" the case. We pray with our whole selves, "thy Kingdom come," as an expression of our faithfulness, not to "what is," but to "what is not but could be, should be, and, we trust, will be" the case, that fine day when, indeed, the Kingdom comes.

Along these lines, allow me to call your attention to the famous passage from Hebrews 11:1, in which we read: "Faith is the assurance of things hoped for, the conviction of things not seen."[8] Here faith, or faithfulness, or what might be called "being true to . . . ," is not oriented towards "what is," but toward a future that "is not yet." Hope is future oriented; I do not hope for what is, but for what might be. The reference here to that which is not seen does not refer to something that is real but just invisible to us; it is not seen because it is not yet; it is still in the future, still to come. We *see* "what is"; we *envision* "what is not," what we cannot yet see. In Jesus's references to the Kingdom of God we are pointed not to the way that things "are," but to the way that things "should be." This orientation toward the Kingdom, toward God's faithfulness in his

8. Heb 1:11 (NRSV).

promise of the Kingdom, and our faithfulness in participating in its coming, is what the Bible means by truth.

So, when we read in John 8:32 (NRSV)—"And you will know the truth, and the truth will set you free"—what is this truth that will make us free? On the interpretation I am offering, I take this to mean not that there is some piece of knowledge, even total knowledge, that, when we learn it, will set us free; rather, the truth sets us free in that it liberates us from the ways of the world that enslave us. The truth sets us free from "what is," from the facts, as we are faithful to, true to, the redemptive vision of "what is not, but could be, and should be," instead. To be animated by that vision is to know the truth, in the richest, Biblical sense of the word.

6. Conclusion

So, where have we gotten? So far, I have outlined the current crisis in truth that is popularly referred to as "the post-truth" era. I have tried to suggest to you that, despite this crisis in truth, truth still matters, and it matters a lot, to each of us personally, and to us collectively. We rightly distrust what passes as truth today, but we still need the truth, and long for it. I then presented a picture of the predominant way in which we understand truth today (truth as facts), contrasted that with a richer view of truth (truth as faithfulness), and then indicated that it is the latter, rather than the former, sense of truth that is of central concern in the Scriptures, and that should be of central concern to us in our Christian lives.

In what remains, I hope, in the second chapter, to make the case that the crisis in truth we are experiencing today has as one of its principal causes the fact that we moderns, even we modern Christians, have understood truth as a matter of fact rather than as a matter of faithfulness, and to give some account of how that came about, and, in the third chapter, to examine what all of this means for the task of the Christian university.[9]

---

9. My hope is that what is envisioned in chapter three for the Christian university can be extrapolated, *mutatis mutandis*, to other Christian institutions and communities.

CHAPTER 2

ALTERNATIVE FACTS: WORLDVIEWS AND TRUTH

1. Alternative facts

AFTER THE 2016 U.S. presidential inauguration, Donald Trump had his Press Secretary, Sean Spicer, brag that the crowd for President Trump's inauguration was the largest ever, larger even than President Obama's historic crowd had been eight years earlier. Mr. Spicer made this claim with belligerent enthusiasm, and with a straight face, despite the fact that there were photographs that clearly showed that there were significant empty areas on the lawns between the capital building and the Lincoln Memorial for Trump's inauguration that were full for Obama's. When later confronted with this evidence, White House advisor Kellyanne Conway provided the following infamous response: "Sean Spicer, our Press Secretary, gave alternative facts to that."[1]

Detractors of the Trump administration flew into an outrage at the insistence upon this obvious and shameless falsehood, and the President countered by accusing anyone who contradicted his account of just about anything at all of "fake news." Thus the age of alternative facts (already well underway) came into full bloom, each side of the political spectrum picking and choosing, spinning and inventing evidence that supported its preferred

1. Todd and Conway, *Conway: Press Secretary Gave 'Alternative Facts'*. Accessed October 27, 2021.

conclusions, and refuting or simply ignoring anything that supported the case on the other side. "*The* truth" has dissolved into Trump's truth versus the media's truth, liberal truth versus conservative truth, women's truth versus men's truth, my truth versus your truth, which is pretty much the death knell for the "truth itself" (if there even is such a thing).

Kellyanne Conway's comment in particular, and the outrageous political climate in the United States in general, sparked a series of promotional spots on and for the CNN television network that sought, at once, to counter the Trump teams' flouting of the truth, and to suggest that if you wanted to know the truth, rather than Trump's lies, then you needed to tune in to CNN. One of the earliest of these ads showed an apple along with this commentary: "This is an apple. Some people might try to tell you that it's a banana. They might scream 'banana, banana, banana,' over and over and over again. They might put 'BANANA' in all caps. You might even start to believe that this is a banana. But it's not. This is an apple," followed by the visual tagline: "Facts First. . . . CNN."[2] But was CNN really going to present the objective, neutral facts, or were they too caught up in the game, and simply offering their own version of the truth, their own alternative facts? Trump supporters regularly accused CNN and several other news outlets of consistently underreporting the Trump administration's accomplishments while obsessing over accusations that cast President Trump in a negative light. But if *everybody* has an angle, if what we understand the truth to be is a function of our prejudices, what becomes of truth?

2. Non-teleological science

Okay, let us get real. Either Trump's crowd was larger or it was not; there is not a lot of room for ambiguity or argument here, especially when the evidence is right before our eyes. The facts are the facts, right? Trump is lying, either for political purposes, or because his ego is so big that it is eclipsing his sight lines to

2. CNN, "Facts First" Twitter Post. https://twitter.com/CNN/status/9224 02297581375488. Accessed October 27, 2021.

the photos giving clear evidence of his smaller crowd. Or else, as some in his administration have claimed, the photos were taken at the wrong time, from slightly different angles, deceptively chosen by the Democratic-leaning, fake media to mislead the American people. In either case, is not CNN right? What we need are the facts, the facts first, and we can work from there.

For most of the "educated" world, that is, for most of us who have received a good, mainstream education, and who benefit from the economic, social, and cultural benefits that accompany such an education, the very idea that there could be "alternative facts" is laughable when it is not simply outrageous. We understand how the scientific method works; we are aware of its built-in safeguards against prejudice; we know that there are not only good, but overwhelmingly compelling reasons why some things are considered true and others false. Scientists are not just making stuff up; professors are not just flipping coins; researchers do not just get the results they want. The facts *are* the facts, right? But that way of thinking is neither universal (that is, it is not shared by everybody), nor does it come from nowhere.

Okay, I have been trying to avoid it, but the time has come to look at a little bit of the history of philosophy. Not much, and not very deeply, but enough hopefully that we can begin to understand *why* we understand things the way that we do—which is not a bad description of what philosophy is all about. Roughly four centuries ago, in the 1600s, something happened that, almost literally, but certainly profoundly, changed the world, and like most significant changes, this one had a very good side to it, and also a very dangerous side to it. So, what happened?

Prior to this time, our understanding of things was what is called "teleological." The word "*telos*" is a Greek word which means "meaning," or "purpose." We often translate it as "end," in the sense of the "end" at which we are aiming in making use of something. So, the *telos* (the purpose, the meaning, the end) of a knife is for cutting, the *telos* of a chair is for sitting, the *telos* of a comb is for fixing one's hair, which is why your bald friend does not need one. On the traditional view of things, understanding something *included* an understanding of what the end, or purpose, of the thing was. If I told my students that I understood what a hat was, and I was able to provide them with a very accurate description of a hat down to its chemical composition, but then proceeded to pull it onto my foot and walk to class, they would probably turn to each other and say: "Well, we knew it was going to happen at some point, but Dudiak has finally lost it. He no longer even understands what a hat is." On the classical view, that is, in Western (that is, Eurocentric) thought from the classical Greeks two-thousand-five-hundred years ago on down to about four-hundred years ago, including the idea of teleology as part of our understanding did not only apply to man-made things like knives and chairs and combs and hats, but also to everything in nature: I only really understood an apple when I understood its *telos*, what it was *for*, that it was good *for* eating; I really only understood water when I understood that it was *for* drinking, or *for* swimming in, especially if you are a fish; and I only really understood the stars when I understood them as mood-setting backlighting *for* romantic kisses, though perhaps they serve some other cosmic functions as well.

That is, the understanding of what something "is," the facts about it, included an understanding of its place in some larger story, some context in which it made sense and had the meaning that it did. In the Middle Ages, prior to the modern era that we are in the course of describing, a lot of ethics was related to this idea, in something called "natural law theory" that still has an effect on the way that some of us think, especially, interestingly, on sexual matters.[3] On this view, the *purpose* of the thing, which is part of what something *is*, determines how the thing should be used. Women, on this view, are clearly designed to bear children, so that is what, on this view, women are *for*, and that determines their role and place in society. The *telos*, the purpose, of sexual activity, on this

3. Though not exclusively, of course. Another obvious area where "natural law theory" is still influential is in the area of "natural human rights." A human being simply by dint of being a human being has certain inalienable rights, something that John Locke, perhaps above all others, emphasized in the seventeenth century (for Locke these rights were life, liberty and property) and that has made its way into the thinking and constitutions of western democracies.

view, is conceiving children, and so engaging in sexual activity for any other purpose, say, for fun, is wrong, because it goes against the *purpose* of sexual activity. (Of course, it was okay if having fun was a side-effect of sexual activity which was being engaged in for the purposes of conceiving children, but that could not be its *purpose*.) This teleological notion is also part of why homosexual activity was considered wrong; it was sex that could not result in conception, and so was contrary to the very purpose of sex. And so with everything in nature, and in every area of life, well beyond just sexual stuff. God had made things with a purpose, or so this story goes, and we understood them when we understood their purpose, and we were obedient to God when we used them according to the purposes God created them to have.[4]

What emerged in the seventeenth century were two interdependent factors that reinforced each other and, over time, created a thought and life world that we refer to as "modernism," as distinguished from the preceding "medieval" thought and life world. On the one hand, the old, standard story about the meaning of things which had ruled in the Middle Ages under the leadership of church-state co-operative was beginning to show some cracks, as the Renaissance in the fifteenth century (reviving the works of a pre-Christian, pagan world) and the Reformation in the sixteenth century (challenging the unified authority of the Church as governing access to salvation) offered alternatives to the ruling narrative, and the old authorities, traditions, and myths suddenly appeared less self-evident. Suddenly, it was not quite so clear that what we had for so very long believed, taught by the church and supported by the secular authorities, was entirely true. Contributing to, and being supported by, this skepticism there emerged a new vision for doing what at the time was called "natural philosophy," but that we today refer to as "natural science," one that relied less upon authoritative statements from the ancients and more upon empirical, that is experiential and experimental, evidence,

---

4. Please note: I am not advocating for the positions put forth in this paragraph—only illustrating how the being of a thing and its meaning were, prior to the modern period, understood as necessarily interconnected.

made possible across the development of what we now refer to as the scientific method.

One of the things that was central to this new way of engaging in natural philosophy was that it was becoming more practical, or, as we say in philosophy, "instrumentalist" (meaning that science is used as an instrument to something else, to achieving something). The goal of the new science was not so much "understanding," of finding something's place and one's place alongside of it, but "prediction and control," accomplished, in words attributed to the early modern philosopher Francis Bacon, by putting "nature on the rack," or "torturing nature to reveal her secrets."[5] In order to predict what something would do, and thus exercise control over what would happen, it was not necessary to understand what something was, in the sense of the role it played in some larger story, but only to understand what immediately caused it, so that that cause could be repeated with the same result. This new way of doing science no longer concerned itself with teleology, with the meaning or purpose of things, but only with the chains of causes and effects that brought things to be and governed their effects upon each other. The scientific explanation of an apple, then, consisted of delineating the causes (physical, chemical, biological) of an apple; that an apple is good to eat is fortunate, but no part of its scientific explanation.[6]

Most early modern, natural philosophers were of the mind that by proceeding in this way they were isolating *a particular way of producing certain kinds of truths for very specific purposes.* That is, they understood that science was really good at identifying a certain kind of truth, but that there were lots of other kinds of truth that science was not able to arrive at. As time went on, and as this way of doing science became increasingly successful

5. That these words were not actually those of Bacon, but attributed to him by later thinkers, is maintained in: Pesic, "Proteus Rebound," 304–17. Whether Bacon's words or not, these phrases capture the "over against," even "confrontational," attitude of many early modern scientists towards their objects of study.

6. Of course, that an apple is good to eat might play a role in some other causal chain, like explaining its role in evolution or in economics, etc.

at prediction and control, *the kinds of truths that these natural philosophers were producing began to be considered not only truths of a particular kind, but the very measure of truth itself.* By the late eighteenth century, modern thinking was becoming what was beginning to be called "Enlightenment" thinking, which was both the popularization and the absolutizing of modern scientific ways of thinking. If, for the early moderns, science was a particular way of producing a certain kind of truth, in the Enlightenment the truths that science produced became the standard for truth itself, indeed, for many, *the* exclusive way of arriving at truth. At once, truth was disconnected from teleology, that is, from any larger story about what the meaning of things was, and science became the only way of arriving at the truth.

What is left? Well, pure facts. What do they mean? Well, nothing, they just are. The fact that energy equals mass times the speed of light squared does not serve any purpose, is not the means to some end, it is just the way it is. This is an apple. It does not matter what story you are trying to tell, it is still an apple. Facts first. Facts standing on their own. Facts have been severed from meaning and purpose. There just are the facts. *End of story.*

But listen carefully to what I just said. For if stories, what the moderns in derision called myths[7], are the meaning context for facts, are what allow us to understand facts within a particular perspective, the modernist/Enlightenment claim is that stories play no role in determining the truth, and so modernity is quite literally the *"end of the story,"* or at least the *end of the relationship between stories and truth.* This is why when you are taking a physics class you think that you are learning the truth about the world, but when you are studying a novel in your English course you think you are engaged with "fiction," which is defined as something that is not true. In science you are studying truth; in English somebody is just making crap up. (And in philosophy not only are we making up crap, we are making up crap that nobody understands!) But notice that in order to arrive at the conclusion that science operates independently of stories we had to follow

7. The Greek word *mythos* simply means "story."

out a particular modernist story about science and its relationship to truth. The idea that facts can be isolated from larger meaning contexts is itself the *end of a story*, is the conclusion of a story that moderns like to tell. So modernity has its own story after all, though, ironically, a story about why it does not need stories. The idea that facts are independent of teleology is not itself a fact, but part of a story that modern, Enlightenment thinkers tell about facts, about science and what it "means."

So maybe facts are not really independent, isolated things after all. Maybe facts are necessarily related to some way of understanding them, that gives them the meaning that we take them as having. Maybe our way of understanding the facts affects what the facts mean to us, and in this way affects the facts themselves, even what we understand to be facts in the first place. But that goes against the dogma about the tight interrelationship between truth and facts and science that we—almost all of us in modern, educated society—accept. Maybe truth is more complicated than we think. But if that is the case, does not that land us right back in the middle of the post-truth problem that we discussed in the previous chapter? If the truth is not simply the truth, but is related to how we see the world—if what we take to be true depends on the stories we tell about it—is the truth then just anything we want it to be? Does not that just make a joke out of the very idea of *the* truth? Then there really *are* alternative facts. Could Kellyanne Conway be right, after all?

3. Distrusting truth

Before we move on, I want to make the problem even more complex, for not only is there a theoretical problem with the claim that facts are the sole arbiter of truth, that is, that facts and truth are the same thing, there is a practical, that is an "ethical," problem with this claim as well.

To illustrate this, let me tell you a brief story. When I was an undergraduate student at Malone College (now University) in northeastern Ohio, I used to drive most weekends about an hour away to help out at a small Quaker church. I was something like an unofficial youth pastor (where unofficial means unpaid). I came to love the folks there, who were very sincere, and very warm, and who even taught this up-tight Canadian how to hug— though I have largely repented of that practice since. Even then, in the early 1980s, times in central Ohio were hard. The factories were already closing, and a good proportion of the men in the congregation were unemployed, or at least underemployed. Downtowns of formerly vibrant communities were closing down and becoming desolate and dangerous. There were few prospects for young people. Those kids with a spark went away to college or university, and never came back. For others, only the military seemed to offer a way out. Still others languished. Many of these good people had little and were headed for less. Yet they clung, as best they could, to family and faith, and, despite being largely ignored by the movers and shakers in the far-away centers of power, they remained staunchly patriotic.

That was forty years ago, and nothing has gotten much better. While over the past two generations, rapid, unprecedented, technological progress and economic growth has been the watchword for much of the continent, while the more "educated" areas of the continent prospered from the shift from industrialization to financial services to the information economy, while the Dow Jones Industrials soared, skyrocketing those who had a lot into those who had even more, and expanding the wealth gap over those who could not afford to invest in the markets, while the "elites" on the coasts (the name those I am speaking about give to those who are benefitting from "the facts") sent their kids to private schools so that the next generation could profit even more from the ever-widening privilege divide, many of the kids I worked with in the youth group in Salem, Ohio, are still there, now in their forties or fifties, waiting for things to get better for them, too. But, if recent history is any indication, it does not look good. So they voted for Donald Trump. Why? Because they *need* alternative facts. Because "the truth," which is controlled by the educated classes, has simply not worked for them.

The *fact* is that the coal industry is dead in the water, both from an environmental and an economic perspective—regardless of whatever nostalgia exists for the days when a blackened face meant green in your pocket. The *fact* is that American manufacturing cannot compete with lower-cost foreign competition—something that tariffs are not going to fix. The *fact* is that the shrinking tax base in middle-American cities and towns cannot support the infrastructure requirements for a stable and healthy life for their residents. The *fact* is that it is easier and more profitable for modern industries to draw the talent out of such areas than to invest in them. The *fact* is that the "rust belt" areas of which I speak have no realistic prospects for substantial, immediate regeneration regardless of what politicians on either side promise. No wonder the good people from these areas are attracted to alternative facts, facts other than those from which the "elites" are profiting, and that are leaving them behind. They have been betrayed by "the facts." Why should they be faithful to the facts? The truth does not work for them, but against them. It is not *their* truth, so why should they believe it?

So when the "educated" classes come along and speak condescendingly to them, when the educated classes, with their fancy degrees and scientific facts, come along and tell them that their whole way of life is backward, that they are "uneducated" "deplorables,"[8] that they are disciplining their children wrong, that the nuclear family is up for grabs, that their religious beliefs are nonsense, should it be any huge surprise that they are not all that impressed with "the truth"? It is easy for the educated classes to advocate for the truth understood in the modernist sense, because they are benefitting from it. But for those for whom "the truth" in this sense is a betrayal of the way of life they hold dear, for those to whom "the truth" has proven unfaithful, we should not be surprised that they would not be too impressed by the truth, and opt for another truth, a truth that would be true, or faithful, to them, too. They

8. As Hilary Clinton once infamously and unfortunately put it. For more information about this controversy, see Merica and Tatum, "Clinton Expresses Regret." Accessed October 27, 2021.

are attracted to alternative facts, or reject the idea of the truth altogether, much to the disdain of the educated classes who think that these folks are just stubbornly rejecting the plain, objective facts—not realizing that their own facts are connected to a story too, and that they are benefitting from such facts at the expense of others. So science gets pitted against religion, intellectual sophistication gets pitted against good, old-fashioned common sense, the coasts get pitted against the middle, blue states against red states, urban against rural, each side cherry picking their own facts as much to counter the other side as to support their own, resulting in the kind of political polarization we see today. Which is yet another reason why the post-truth era is in full swing.

4. Christian worldview and alternative facts?

Anyone who has spent any significant period of time around the North American Christian college scene will have heard the phrase "Christian worldview" used with considerable regularity and often with evangelistic zeal. The term "worldview" was taken over from early twentieth-century German philosophy, in which language it sounds much cooler: *Weltanschauung!* The term literally means "the way in which we view the world," the idea being that *how we see things, the way in which we see things, affects what we see.* "Seeing," here, does not mean physical sight so much as it means "understanding" in the sense that when I finally understand something I exclaim: "Oh, I see!" Having a particular worldview means that I, along with the group to which I belong and with whom I share this worldview, understand the world in a particular way, "see" things in one way rather than in another, and that I live my life in some particular way that stems out of the meaning that I understand the world to have. "Worldview" should, therefore, be understood in a broad way, because our "understanding" of the world both stems from and affects every aspect of our lives—intellectual, yes, but also the emotional, corporeal, ethical, and spiritual aspects of who we are. Our worldview affects who we take ourselves to be and in what kind of world we take ourselves to live, affects what we understand reality—and our place in it—to be.

In terms of what I have been talking about so far in this chapter, worldviews can be understood as the stories that we tell ourselves about the meaning of things in general, and that affect how we understand things in particular.

That might be a little abstract, so let me give you an example: the idea of "creation." At least at The King's University where I teach (and I suspect in very many other Christian institutions as well), from biology classes to sociology courses to theology classes and beyond, you will find that what in other places might be called "nature" or "the world" or "all of reality," at King's is referred to as "creation." Now, when you hear one of us at King's referring to "creation," we are not primarily talking about how the world came to be, as in the argument between creation and evolution. That is, when we talk about "creation," most of the time we are not referring to some "fact" about the origins of the world; rather, we are talking about *a way of seeing the world* in its entirety. Creation, that is, is not a word that refers to a "fact" (which is the way it is taken by those who engage in the argument between creation and evolution); rather, it is a worldview term—it speaks about a way of seeing, a way of understanding, what the facts (whatever they may be) ultimately mean. When we speak about "creation," we are saying that we understand *everything that is* in relationship to God, and that that relationship determines the meaning of everything that is. It is our way of saying that we do not understand the universe as the product of some random events that are ultimately meaningless, and that meaning is just an expression of human preference. Rather, everything that is, as created by God, has meaning, has purpose. "It is good!" is the affirmation we read over and again in the creation story in Genesis. As the creatures charged with "Lordship" over creation (that is, who are called to emulate in our attitude toward creation the attitude that *our Lord* the suffering servant has toward us), we human beings are called to responsibility for the whole of creation. Everything that *is* is a gift to us, but not for us to use however we like, as we are responsible for everything that is, too. "Creation" does not name a fact so much as it names a perspective on things, an attitude, with an attendant responsibility.

To understand reality as creation, to live within the Christian story, is to understand all that is as a gift from God for which we are responsible, which is a very different understanding of all that is from the secularist, Enlightenment understanding of things as the arbitrary outcome of random processes without inherent meaning or purpose. That is, understanding the world *as* God's creation reveals to us a different reality than understanding the world *as* the product of ultimately random events. Or, put otherwise, what something means is built into the reality of that thing, and not something added "after the fact." Things in the world are actually different kinds of things according to these different ways of understanding: on the Christian worldview, human beings are made in the image of God, whereas on the secularist worldview we are only very sophisticated animals. Since we are actually dealing with different kinds of things in each case, our understanding of them, and the facts about them, will also be different, as will also be our responsibilities toward them. To understand ourselves as one or the other is, in a certain sense, to be dealing with a different reality, to be living in "a different world." While the same science "works" for each of these worldviews— Christian scientists can employ the same formulae to predict and control creation that secular scientists use to predict and control nature—science itself means something different in each case, as *a particular, and very useful, perspective* on a richer reality, in the case of a Christian worldview, and as the *privileged and only legitimate access to truth* on a scientistic worldview.

But if a Christian worldview in a certain important sense gives us access to a different world than the one on offer on a secularist worldview, and the things found in each of these alternative worlds are in fact different than they are in the other, are we then—Christians in general, but Christian universities in particular—complicit in the dangerous prospect of arguing for "alternative facts" that threatens the integrity of truth in our post-truth age? That is, are we, with our worldview talk, part of the problem?

5. Worldviews vs. ideologies

Obviously, the concern over "alternative facts" is that our world-views keep us from seeing the facts about things, keep us from recognizing and acknowledging the truth about things—keep us locked within the limited and distorted perspectives of our prejudices. The conviction of the former American president and his circle that he is the greatest person who ever walked the earth means that his inauguration crowd must also have been the biggest, and if "the photographic facts" do not line up with this prejudice (which means "pre-judgement") then the facts must be wrong, and alternative facts need to be created to fit with this prejudice. Similarly, those who see their accumulation of wealth threatened by environmental regulations are forced to deny "the physiochemical facts" of global warming, and to create their own facts to account for the data. Likewise, those who believe that the world was created 6,000 years ago in seven days must deny "the geological facts" pointing to a world billions of years old and find a different way of accounting for fossils.

In philosophy, in politics, and in other discourses too, we have a word for this phenomenon where a prejudice keeps us from seeing the truth: "ideology." The word "ideology" contains as its root the word "idea;" so here, my prior idea about something keeps me from acknowledging the facts that would contradict my idea. Being accused of having an ideology is thus a pejorative thing, an insult; it means that your prejudice blinds you to the truth. My idea of myself is that I am profoundly fashionable in the most classical sense, and that keeps me from acknowledging the fact that my students are laughing at my eccentric wardrobe, which clearly needs a serious update. Donald Trump's ego-driven ideas about himself keep him from being able to see that his in-auguration crowd was smaller than Obama's. The idea that the Bible should always be interpreted literally keeps certain Chris-tians from recognizing as true many broadly-accepted scientific facts. In each case, or so the story goes, there is a truth about things, but my prejudice, my ideology, keeps me from seeing it. So no one wants to be thought of as having an ideology; no one wants to be thought of as having prejudices that blind them to the truth that is right in front of them.

But have I not just been arguing that our worldviews to some large extent affect what we understand reality to be, and thus the facts about the world that come into view by means of them? Have I not also just argued that modern secularism with its ultimate trust in science is as much a worldview as is the Christian worldview? Are we then stuck with alternative facts because we are stuck with alternative worldviews, that is, alternative ideologies? Do "they" have their facts while "we" have our own, alternative facts, after all? That is, are our different worldviews really just different ideologies, such that we are, all of us, stuck within our own prejudices?

What I want to suggest to you is that there is actually a difference between worldviews and ideologies. Allow me to put it this way: if an ideology is a way of understanding the world that keeps me from accessing the "richness" of what is "out there" for me to see, a worldview opens up my understanding of what is "out there" and allows me to see it in ever deeper and more helpful ways. If the former President south of the border could see past his ego, he could recognize that there are other people beyond him with interests and ideas beyond his own that have validity and that are also important, and in doing so he could enrich his world and his capacity to function well within it. If the absolutization of the profit motive could be challenged then industrialists could recognize that living richly means much more than simply having money in their several bank accounts and a well-balanced stock portfolio, but that clean air and water and earth for subsequent generations might be the greatest investment of all. Likewise, if I could just admit that it is the 2020s and no longer the 1920s, then maybe I could open myself up to new fashion possibilities and finally slip, however uncomfortably, into the twenty-first century.

Everyone, every group, has a worldview, a story, a lens through which to understand reality, and a manner of being immersed within it and interacting with it, but sometimes a worldview can degenerate into an ideology, which can happen to a Christian worldview too. An ideology is a kind of ossified worldview, a way of seeing the world and being in the world that is rigid and stuck in its ways. An ideology is a lens that does not open up reality, allowing us to see it and engage it in ever more insightful and exciting ways, but a distorting lens that eclipses unwanted insights, closes us off from reality and its possibilities. An ideology is a way of seeing the world that cannot see beyond its own way of seeing, that is incapable of seeing anything new or unexpected, anything interesting or challenging. A healthy worldview is a lens that perpetually opens reality up, provides a way of being in the world that does not impose its own expectations upon reality, but is open to what is beyond its own expectations, seeing what it has not yet seen, considering ever new possibilities.

This means that a healthy worldview needs *itself* to be susceptible to being opened up always and again, to being perpetually formed and re-formed in light of what it opens upon, to changing and growing and evolving. When I see something that challenges my expectations, I may need to adjust my way of seeing itself. A healthy worldview is the embodiment of an open-ended story, always being re-written in light of the emergence of unanticipated situations, eccentric characters, emerging realities, fresh possibilities. You will recall from chapter one that, for Christians, the truth is not equivalent with the facts, with "what is," but includes also reference to "what should be the case, to what we are called to make real, but that is not yet real" (or at least not as fully real as it might be). But that means that "what is not yet real" is not itself just some set of facts that has yet to be realized, something that functions in the mode of "what is" even if it is "not yet." In a healthy, Christian worldview, we are open to the unexpected, even beyond "orthodox" Christian expectation, open to God's surprising creative and re-creative acts, to the redemption and re-generation even of our worldview itself. A healthy Christian worldview cannot be a finished product, a set of doctrinal "facts" that limit in advance what being faithful might mean, because that which "is not" disrupts and judges what "is," even what "is" at present understood to be the Christian worldview.

Therefore, facts do not exist on their own, but are instead embedded in a worldview in terms of which they become the facts that they are. But neither are facts just the product of some worldview or another such that we are justified in ignoring the facts we do not like. We see through a lens that opens up a world to us which in turn affects the nature of the lens itself, which then opens up the world in a richer way, which again affects how we see, and so on and so on, *ad infinitum*, as our Latin friends might say. A healthy worldview does not overpower the facts, nor is it a slave to the facts. A healthy Christian worldview does not require us to deny the science of evolution because we have our own, alternative facts, nor must we abandon our Christian worldview because we are convinced by evolution. Rather, our Christian worldview should allow us to be open to the facts that present themselves to us in ways that allow our Christian worldview itself to become enriched, even while our Christian worldview allows us to cast the facts in new and exciting ways that bring fresh insight and new possibilities for both understanding and redeeming our world.

Our worldviews, at their healthiest, do not only open up the world of facts to us in ever richer and endlessly fascinating and exciting ways, they are also the embodiment of a way of being faithful. The truth of a worldview is not measured only by its ability to connect us with the world of facts, but is measured also by its capacity to employ those facts in the cause of an ever deepening faithfulness. So, what *is* the truth? Are the hungry fed? Do the lame walk? Are the naked clothed? Are we stewarding creation? Are the good people of Salem, Ohio, waking up in the morning with hope?

As we have learned already, there is much more to truth than the facts, which is why at the Christian university we need to spend significant time and devote adequate resources not only to teaching the facts, but inviting students into a Christian worldview, into a way of understanding and being in the world, that—while always open to being enriched, corrected, reformed—we believe is *true*, which means, that it is an embodiment of our faithfulness to that to which God calls us. I will explore these ideas further in the following chapter on truth in the Christian university.

CHAPTER 3

YOURS TRULY: TRUTH AND
THE CHRISTIAN UNIVERSITY

1. Knowing and knowing about

THE UNIVERSITY IS IN the knowledge business, and what we hope to come to know in our pursuit of knowledge is the truth about things. One of my colleagues at The King's University, Dr. Chris Peet, tells the story of spending a whole class providing a schematic of the history of Western intellectual thought on the board, and at the end of the class a young woman put her hand up and asked: "Dr. Peet, is that true, or did you make it up?" I know Dr. Peet, who is a good friend of mine, and he probably made it up. But the point is that students do not go to university to learn things that are false, but things that are true. In fact, if Dr. Peet were, for instance, teaching our students that Napoleon's commissioning of the King's James Bible was a key turning point in the high Middle Ages, and students were to believe him, they could not be said to have any real knowledge at all, and they would be fully justified in asking the university president for their tuition money back. As early as Plato, Western philosophy has defined "knowledge" as "justified *true* belief,"[1] a phrase we will not analyze now other than to point out that knowledge *means* knowledge of the truth, that the two ideas are necessarily linked.

---

1. Bunryeat, Levett, and Plato, *Theaetetus*, 201 c–d.

So the university, both in its research and teaching capacities, is in the knowledge business, which means that it is in the truth business. If it is the case, as I am arguing in this little book, that truth most fundamentally *means* faithfulness, then the task of the Christian university cannot be the bare pursuit of the facts, but *must be a faithful pursuit of the facts*.

Consider this: if knowledge is the knowledge of truth, and what we are considering in this study is a richer idea of what truth is, we should not be too surprised to discover that there is available to us a richer idea of knowledge too, one that corresponds to this richer idea of truth, and that like the richer idea of truth, has also been eclipsed by the modern reduction of truth to the results of scientific research. If there is a kind of knowledge that corresponds to truth as fact—for to know the facts is to arrive at a certain kind of truth—might there also be a kind of knowledge that corresponds to truth as faithfulness?

Many of you will no doubt be familiar with the famous phrase in the Bible: "Adam *knew* his wife Eve and they conceived a child." Now, when Adam *knew* his wife Eve and they conceived a child, they were not exchanging information, they were not exchanging facts, . . . they were exchanging bodily fluids. When I was a kid, growing up in a quite conservative church environment, this phrase was the cause of considerable, naughty hilarity. "Do you know Jane?" someone might ask, to which the response was, "Yes, but not Biblically." In other contexts, this kind of knowledge—the way that Adam "knew" Eve—was called "carnal" (that is, "bodily") knowledge, in distinction from "intellectual" knowledge. The distinction here is, however, not best thought of as a distinction between mind and body. Rather, the way that Adam knew Eve—as opposed to the way that we generally use the term "know" today—refers to their *intimate familiarity*.

We also use the term knowledge in this way outside of sexual contexts. If I were, for example, to take an hour or two and tell you everything I could think of about my mom, and then I were to ask you, "Do you know my mom?," most of you would say something like, "Well, I know a lot *about* your mom, but I do not *know* her. I have never met her." You might know facts about my mom, even many important ones, but you have no familiarity with her, no intimacy with her. You would have *knowledge about* her, but you would not *know* her.

So there is a difference between knowledge as "knowing about," and knowledge as "intimate familiarity." Now, the modern university specializes in "knowledge about," almost to the exclusion of "knowledge as intimate familiarity," and that has become particularly true over the past two centuries wherein the modern university has become focused on "research," an emphasis that pervades the contemporary university, including Christian universities, where faculty need to engage in both teaching and research. But note that "research" implies a certain kind of knowledge acquisition, and thus a certain kind of knowledge, and, as I am suggesting, a certain kind of truth. In research I am "searching" for something that is out there, independent of me, preferably with the aid of laboratories and protocols and statistics. In the modern university, real knowledge is the knowledge that science provides, and other kinds of knowledge do not really cut it. In fact, they are not really considered knowledge at all. Having coffee with my mom might be a pleasant way to pass an afternoon (or not), but under normal circumstances that would not be considered scientific activity, would not yield systematic knowledge. If, however, I analyzed her DNA, well, then I would have knowledge.

Notice something important here; the key to "knowing about" is keeping my distance. We call this "objectivity," where what I know is the *object "out there"* unaffected by me, the knowing *subject*, who needs to be taken out of play in the process of knowledge acquisition. This is, indeed, the whole point of the modern scientific method! It does not matter who you are, or where you are, or your creed or race or gender, you should get the same result, because science is not about you, it is about what you are studying. If you are personally involved in the process, if you have an interest in the outcome, you cannot be objective, and the results of your study cannot be trusted to provide real knowledge, and genuine truth. The pursuit of such objective, arm's-length truth is the very stock in trade of the modern university, what it aims at, what it brags about, and it jealously guards its monopoly on knowledge from any claims to truth that *do not measure up* to its standard—quite literally, that cannot be objectively *measured*!

But notice that when it comes to knowledge in the sense of intimate familiarity, precisely the opposite is the case: it is impossible to keep my distance. Adam and Eve could not "know" each other "in the Biblical sense" at a distance, rather—if you will excuse me for putting it this way—the first couple had to be totally into each other! Likewise, if you are to get to know your friends in this sense of knowledge, if you are to grow your intimacy with your friends, you have to care deeply about your friends, be fully there, open yourself up to them, let them in, be vulnerable, tread compassionately amongst their vulnerabilities, be fully involved with them. In a relationship of intimate familiarity, what happens to them affects you deeply, and your being affected by their situation affects them in turn, because in intimate familiarity friends are a part of each other—what concerns one concerns both. I want to suggest to you further—and if I am right about this, this is extremely important—that *when the Bible talks about knowledge, and particularly when it speaks of knowing God, what it is predominantly and overwhelmingly talking about is not knowledge in the sense of "knowing about," but knowledge in the sense of "intimate familiarity."* You do not *know* God when you know *about* God, when you have aced your catechism class and can navigate the doctrines of the church with scholastic wizardry. You only really *know* God when you are personally involved with God, when you are growing in intimacy with God, when you are fully there, open yourself up, are vulnerable, when you ground your life in God and allow God to live in and through you—in short, to love and be loved by God.

Let me be clear; "knowledge as intimate familiarity" is *not a substitute* for "knowing about"; it is *the context for* knowing about. It is *not* that we *either* have "knowledge as intimate familiarity" *or* we have "knowledge about." Rather, "knowing about" is *one aspect* of "knowledge as intimate familiarity," just as the truth of facts is one kind of truth, one kind of faithfulness. Doctrines are not unimportant, but they are *expressions* of a deeper knowledge of God, the knowledge of intimate familiarity to which the Scriptures testify. Likewise, knowing about my mother's DNA is not unimportant, but it is not important for its own sake—it is important because I care about my mother and her health. To analyze my mother's DNA is to abstract from the totality of who she is in order to learn something important about her, but something quite specific. It is similarly a good thing if Adam knows a little bit *about* Eve as part of his *knowing* her in the Biblical sense, that, for instance, she likes to cuddle for a few minutes afterwards, so that he can better grow their intimacy, rather than jumping immediately out of bed to fix himself a snack. (Some of us have learned that lesson the hard way.) Knowing *about*, what we think of primarily as scientific knowledge, is entirely valid; it is an extremely useful abstraction from the richer knowledge that we live every day in our intimate familiarity with other people, with the world, and with God—but it is not the whole of knowledge, and it is not the primary, and especially not the sole, arbiter of truth.

So you can see what I am doing here. If "knowledge about," at the apogee of which sits scientific knowledge, corresponds to what I am referring to as "truth as fact," then "knowledge as intimate familiarity" should correspond with what I am referring to as "truth as faithfulness." Being faithful to someone or something, being *true* to them, requires of me a supreme commitment; the one to whom I pledge my troth, to whom I promise to be true, has to matter profoundly to me, because in pledging myself to them my very being is at stake; who I am will henceforth be forever changed—for good or for ill, but forever changed. Therefore, being true to someone or something forbids, is precisely antithetical to, the kind of safe, critical distance-taking that is the very essence of the knowledge of facts, of modern scientific knowledge, which insists upon indifference as the guarantor of objectivity. Truth, in the sense of faithfulness, thus requires of us a knowing not of the "knowing about" variety, but a knowledge of intimate familiarity, the kind of all-in, body and soul knowledge with which Adam knew Eve, a knowledge not governed by methodological disinterest designed to yield neutral facts, but a knowledge of the caress, issue of the heart, meant to multiply and enrich life.

All of us who were raised and educated within the modernist context, all of us who have imbibed truth as fact with our mother's milk and been taught throughout our schooling that knowledge simply *means* "knowledge about" (that is, all of us within the modernist context, including Christians), find it hard to even imagine that when the Bible talks about knowledge, and when it talks about truth, it is (for the most part and predominantly) talking about something very different from knowing about facts—that when it speaks of knowledge, it is talking about intimate familiarity, and that when it speaks of truth, it is talking about faithfulness. Taking that in requires a significant shift in our understanding, in our worldview, which is not easy. In fact, it means understanding worldviews themselves as not simply ways of viewing the world, but ways of life, as matters of total commitment and ultimate trust. But if there is validity to this proposition, if it is "true"[2] that knowledge in the Biblical sense is the deeper and more fundamental form of knowledge, and that truth as faithfulness is the deeper and more fundamental sense of truth, then the Christian university cannot be faithful to its calling if its orientation is towards *knowledge about* "truth as facts" alone. Rather, we should be seeking the "knowledge of intimate familiarity" with God and neighbor and the world itself as the context for any and all of our scientific pursuits, of all of our attempts to "know about."

Yet, how are we to seek to be faithful to God and neighbor and creation in any and every pursuit of knowledge? For the rest of this chapter, I want to explore what that might mean for the task of the Christian university across three interrelated trajectories, which I hope might make what I am saying rather abstractly here a little more concrete.

---

2. This reference to "true" refers on the surface to a fact, but thus refers, as I am arguing do all facts, to true in the sense of faithful.

2. Not all facts are true

I once wrote an essay, the thesis of which was the following: to the question, "how many Jews can be fit into a cattle car?," there is no true answer. Most readers will already understand what I am talking about, but just in case (remember this material was first written for undergraduates, including freshmen), allow me to briefly explain. When during the Second World War the Nazi party in Germany made it part of their policy to exterminate all of the Jews, one of the means of transporting the rounded up Jewish people to the camps at which they would be killed was to load them onto train cars designed to carry cattle—itself part of the process of dehumanizing these people so that their murders would seem less atrocious. Now, I do not have proof of this,[3] but I suspect that with the pervertedly meticulous bookkeeping and heartless efficiency with which the Nazis undertook this attempt at genocide they would have had a pretty precise estimate of how many cattle cars would be required to carry out their designs, depending on the number of victims they could expect to apprehend in different parts of the territories they controlled. That is, I suspect that the Nazis figured out, or at least could have, with a fair amount of precision, how many Jews they could fit onto a cattle car, and used that *fact* to their pernicious ends. So, to the question, "how many Jews can be fit onto a cattle car?," there *is* a *correct* answer. But, I maintain, there is no *true* answer. Why not?

Because, or at least I am arguing, truth ultimately *means* faithfulness, and the "fact" of the number of Jews that one can fit onto a cattle car for the purposes of their extermination is a fact in the service of an act that is so utterly a betrayal of every moral imperative, of every decency, of every even remote echo of neighbor love, that it cannot with any integrity be called true at all, despite

3. Although Hannah Arendt strongly suggests something of this sort when she speaks of Eichmann's "difficulty in synchronizing departures and arrivals, the endless worry over wrangling enough rolling stock from the railroad authorities and the Ministry of Transport, over fixing timetables and directing trains to centers with sufficient 'absorptive capacity,' over having enough Jews on hand at the proper time so that no trains would be 'wasted,' . . . " Arendt, *Eichmann in Jerusalem*, 153.

being so very correct. To call such a fact "the truth" is a violation of any truth worthy of the name, because it is a violation of those to whom we are called to be faithful; this "fact" stands at the very antipode of "being true."

This is because, as I have argued, the truth refers beyond itself to that to which it is called to be true, to that to which it must be faithful. Recall in the second chapter how the truths of the educated classes have not served the interests of the less educated classes, how the former's truths have been employed, not as a means of faithfulness to the latter, but as a means of betraying them. My argument is that such truths, which are no doubt verifiable by the protocols of scientific inquiry, cannot be true in the richest sense, in the sense of faithfulness, because they fail to *answer to* that to which we are called to be *true*: to God, to neighbor (in the sense that Jesus defined my neighbor), to the rest of creation, and, indeed, to ourselves. Since we are all in this together, since we are all interdependent, in violating my responsibility to others I am violating also my responsibility to myself—being less than *I* can be, and must be.

We *can* abstract from the richer sense of things and identify isolated facts, and there is a place for that; facts are a part of the truth, and our pursuit of them, in our scientific work, is an exhilarating and essential project. It is good that we come to know *about* things. I am very grateful that the ophthalmologist who operated on my damaged eye a few years back knows *how* the eye works. I am grateful for the perspective that sociologists and psychologists and historians add to my understanding of the turbulent machinations of our present political situation. I have long been fascinated by the mind-blowing, astro-physical investigations of how it is that time slows down the faster one moves, how it is that space is curved, and how the speed of light is absolute, not relative to any fixed point. Facts are not only useful, they are also just super-cool. Exploring and experimenting and learning is among the most satisfying activities one can undertake, a near sure-fire antidote to boredom. A big part of what we do in the university is precisely that.

But in the *Christian* university it cannot be all that we do, or even principally what we do, because we recognize a richer truth, a higher truth, of which truths as facts (as interesting and as useful as they are) are in the service. If we seek the truth, if we seek "Biblical" knowledge, we must always ask to whom, or to what, in our pursuit of facts, we owe our fidelity.

3. Taking truth personally

I fully realize that most of us no longer write letters, but that we communicate by Snapchat or Instagram or Twitter, or whatever new platform for instant and trivial communication has sprung up this week. But once upon a time, and not so very long ago, when you could not afford to call someone on the phone (which was usually the case, since long-distance charges even thirty years ago were prohibitive), you got out a piece of paper and a pen, and you wrote them a letter, put it in an envelope, bought a stamp, put it in the mail and waited two or three weeks for a reply—unless your addressee was overseas, in which case you might hear back in two or three months! Since it took so long to get there, you took your time deciding what to write, and really thought it through, attempting to say what you meant, and say it carefully.

The relative merits of instant over against more deliberate communication aside, I want to call your attention to a piece of the etiquette associated with this lost art that was not only polite, but—if we think it through—also has a lesson to teach us about truth. What I am referring to is the way in which we typically signed off our letters: with the phrase "yours truly," followed by one's signature.

Now, notice the form of the term "true" here, "truly," which is adverbial, which requires a verb, which here is implied. In signing my letter "Yours truly," followed by my signature, I am really saying "*I am* yours truly," or "I am truly *yours*," committing myself to you across what is said in the letter. In signing my letter to you, I am undersigning a letter that contains information, facts, sentiments, committing what the letter contains to you and to your care. In saying "yours truly," I am undersigning, that is guaranteeing, what I have written to you in the content of the letter as being true, as being genuine, backing up what I have written to you with my signature, that is, personally guaranteeing the truth of what I am saying with my very self. "Yours truly, Jeffrey." I commit myself to you, and do so as the pledge for what I have said. What is said does not stand on its own; its truth is backed up, supported, by someone, the author of the letter. *The guarantee of the truth of what is said is personal*, precisely, is *my* faithfulness to *you*, which is why yet another variation of "Yours truly" was "Yours faithfully," because, as we have seen, truth *means* faithfulness.

That personal guarantee, that personal aspect of truth, that grounding of truth in faithfulness, is, moreover, not some optional "extra" added on to truth as fact, but is essential to the truth of facts as well. Indeed, were I to receive a letter providing me with all kinds of information of great importance to me, but that letter was anonymous, I would not know whether or not I could trust the contents of the letter. No one is standing behind the claims made in the letter, which is why I do not trust them, which is why I cannot possibly know if the claims made are true. The same phenomena appear in our courts of law, where evidence based on what someone heard someone else say, which is called "hearsay," is inadmissible. We only accept the testimony if the person who has something to say is there in court, in person, to say it themselves, to back up their facts with a pledge of "yours truly," which in the courts takes the form of swearing (or affirming) "to tell the truth the whole truth and nothing but the truth, so help me God." Even scientific evidence rests upon such a pledge. If someone claims that "science says" something (which is tricky given that science does not have a mouth), we are entirely within our rights in asking, "*who* says?" Which scientist, where, and when? Only when the article in the scientific journal is attributed to someone or someones do we trust what it says. "The chemical fluctuations of rainbow fish in the trees of rural Alberta, *Written by* (that is, backed up by, guaranteed by) Leah Martin, Heather Prior, Vern Peters, and Darcy Visscher." That is the scientific version of "yours truly."

So truth is personal, backed up by a person, guaranteed by a person, undersigned by a person who is willing to stand behind it, and pledge themselves and risk their reputation on what is being said. What is "standing behind something" other than "pledging to be faithful to it"? I said it, and I mean it.

Further, in signing my letters in this way, I am not only being true, or faithful, to what is said, I am being true, or faithful, *to you* in saying it. A letter is offered to a person: "Dear mother," or "Dear Sir," or "My dear brown eyes." "I am truly *yours*," or "faithfully *yours*." I will be true to, or faithful to, *what* is said, but the context for that is that I will be true to, or faithful to, *you, to the one to whom I am writing*. This is true also even with the communication of scientific truths; while the addressee is not made explicit, articles in scientific journals are addressed implicitly to a particular scientific community. We do not publish our truths for the sake of these truths alone, but for the sake of our readers, which is why academics are often quite disappointed that journal articles are so little read. I am offering what I am saying to you, to whom I am promising to be true, to be faithful. If I am genuinely being true, I am not writing to you to hurt you, to deceive you, but to be faithful to you.

What, then, does this mean for the work of the Christian university? It means that our striving to come to the knowledge of *truth* in the most important sense of that term is a profoundly personal enterprise that demands our full commitment and an unrelenting faithfulness. Truth does not stand on its own; it is offered to someone, and our offering it to someone in faithfulness to them is itself the core sense of truth. If I want to know the truth, I need across my truth claim to be faithful to the one to whom I offer it—to God and to neighbor.

4. Imagination, facts, and fantasy

If there *is* a formula for the production of facts (these days we call this the scientific method), there is *no* formula for the forging of faithfulness. As I noted already in the first chapter, when on your wedding day you promise to be faithful to someone, you do not and you cannot know in advance what all that is going to mean, which is precisely why your pledge of faithfulness is required. The marriage contract is painfully thin on details: richer or poorer, sickness or health, better or worse, . . . sign on the dotted line and say your prayers. The course of a marriage is not set out in advance. All that is promised is faithfulness, no matter what. The "what" still has to be worked out, encountered, suffered through, negotiated. Two incomes or one? Kids? How many? What makes your partner happy? Is someone going back to school? How to care for aging parents, or ailing children? How to deal with conflict? How to keep things spicy in the bedroom? Do you get the Jag or take the holiday to Australia? Or do neither so you can help the kids with university? Do you decide to live near the grandchildren or move to climes more friendly to your spouse's arthritis? There is no formula for faithfulness; in a certain sense you have to make it up as you go along. But your marriage cannot be just any arbitrary thing that you want; if it is to be truly a marriage (that is, as we have just seen, something I personally undersign by means of my unflagging commitment), then whatever it is to be—whatever infinite options are open to the couple in their working out their own relationship in fear and trembling—must be qualified by faithfulness.

"I am getting married, what should I do?"

"Be faithful."

"What does that mean?"

"Ah, now the great adventure begins!"

There is no formula for faithfulness. There is no formula for our faithfulness to God, no formula for our faithfulness to our neighbor, no formula for our faithfulness to our fellow creatures. Since what faithfulness means cannot be given in advance, being faithful requires an immense capacity for imagination. We are called to make the Kingdom of God a reality. "Thy Kingdom come" Jesus has taught us to pray, but we need to imagine, and reimagine, and imagine ever again and ever anew what that might look like in the ever-evolving situations we find ourselves in as history breaks ever new ground. If the marriage contract is painfully thin on details, so are the Scriptures. The Bible commands us to be faithful, to love God and neighbor and care for the earth, and tells us some stories about what that looked like in certain situations, and how we as God's people fell well short of it in others, but it does not provide us with a formula. The Bible is far more of a story book than it is a textbook, and it invites us to become part of the unfolding story of the coming Kingdom. Jesus was himself a virulent critic of the attempt to capture faithfulness in a formula, which was the way that the law was understood by some of the Jewish leaders of his day, a law that Jesus did not want to destroy but to fulfill, that is, to bring to life across the liberation of the gospel.

> "On these two commandments hang all the law and the prophets,"[4] Jesus profoundly claimed, "love the Lord your God with all your heart, and with all your soul, and with all your mind[. . .] and the second is like it, love your neighbor as yourself."[5]
>
> "What does that mean?"
>
> "Ah, now the great adventure begins!"

Likewise, there is no formula for what faithfulness means in the context of our calling to be the Christian university. As the university our task is to "know," but as the Christian university our task is to pursue not only knowledge about things, but knowledge about things in the context of our being intimately inter-connected with them as our fellow creatures, to understand them in the first instance across a relationship of care, and responsibility to God, for them. As the university our task is to come to a knowledge of the truth, but as the Christian university our task is to seek the truth of facts in the context of a deeper truth, truth as faithfulness. That is, we come to know the truth not only by identifying what is, but by committing ourselves to what is not, but should be, by envisioning and seeking the Kingdom of God.

> "What does that look like in the context of the Christian university?"
>
> "Ah, now the great adventure begins!"

4. Matt 22:40 (NRSV).
5. Matt 22:36–39 (NRSV).

Notice something important here: the coming Kingdom is not a matter of fact, but a matter of faithfulness; it concerns not "what is," but "what is not." It is not therefore to be thought on the model of facts. The Kingdom of God is not to be thought as some factual reality, not even as some factual reality in the future, such that our task in revealing the truth of things would be to come to know those future facts in the present. The Kingdom of God is not predetermined; is not some set of facts just awaiting to come into reality. Rather, the future is the promise of God's faithfulness to us, and a call to us to be faithful to God, come what may, and within that ever-evolving context to imagine and re-imagine and re-imagine again what the Kingdom of God might be like, and to make it a reality, here, today, and tomorrow, and then again the next day.

And so, the great adventure goes on.[6]

So our task *is* to come to know *about* things, yes! All due deference to the facts of the matter, to what is the case, to learning well, to responsible scholarship, to modern science with all of its awesome powers of prediction and control. Truth as fact matters; Christian scholarship is not about just making things up. But, remember, the facts of the matter do not give us the whole truth of things; things are always becoming what they truly are as their potential for playing their role in the emerging Kingdom of God is brought to light and into reality. That is what it means to really know something, in the Biblical sense—to know each creature as playing its role in the service of God. Things are what they are—so facts matter—but things are *not only* what they are, but also what they could be, should be, might yet be—and so to be true to something, to realize its truth, we must go beyond the facts about it, and strive to bring ever more of its creational potential to fruition. Our task in the Christian university is therefore to respect the facts,

6. That is why prophecy is not soothsaying, predicting the future, but a critical perspective on "what is" in light of a "what is not," in light of the promise of the Kingdom of God. And that is why revelation is not the revelation of some set of facts, like having the teacher's version of the textbook with the answers in the back. What is revealed in revelation is a way of faithfulness, a way forth, in the hope of Shalom.

but not to be too intimidated by them. The "realist," the person who insists that we stick to the facts, ignores the greater part of the truth, and so is not very realistic after all.

I am arguing that in addition to learning *about* things, the task of the Christian university requires as its redemptive context a full flowering of the imagination, and that these two ways of thinking about knowing, and about truth, belong together. We can only open up the pharmaceutical potential of a particular chemical composition if we *know about* its structure and properties; but we only *fully understand* its structure and properties when we understand them against the background of their God-given redemptive potentialities. We can only explore the possibilities of a more just political system if we are realistic *about* the nature of human beings; but we only *fully understand* human beings when we understand ourselves against that to which we are called: to image God, to be good neighbors, to exercise the Lordship that is suffering servanthood. We can only understand a novel if we *know about* literary forms, genres, metaphors, syntax, and character development, but we can only *fully understand* literature when we understand its potential to present us with possible worlds, to challenge us towards compassion for the other, to invite us to play on the boundaries of reality. Fiction, "what is not the case," is, remember, at the heart of the gospel.

Indeed, the possibility of a break with "what is" is built into the Biblical message. Forgiveness is precisely such a break: you have committed the deed, you deserve to suffer the consequences, but . . . miracle of miracles . . . you are forgiven. Forgiveness loosens the bonds between the deed and the consequences so that something new, something undeserved, something contrary to the hard laws of cause and effect, can insinuate itself into things and allow for new life. Forgiveness is a supreme act of the imagination, the ability to envision an outcome contrary to the facts. You have betrayed your friend; you do not deserve to have such a friend; then, you are forgiven, and your friendship is able to move forth creatively and redemptively. Grace names the same phenomenon generalized to all of creation: what is the case does not determine what will be the case; something new can happen, will happen, must happen, something unanticipated, unforeseen, something other than what the deterministic laws of nature dictate, offering new life where life has been suffocated by the perpetual layering of itself upon itself, of the same always upon the same—vanity of vanity, all is vanity—that is, by death. *The break with necessity does not require a miracle, because reality itself is miraculous.* Which is why, as my esteemed colleague in English, Arlette Zinck, has wonderfully put it: "Christians do not do hopeless." Why not? Because the truth is rooted in possibility.

Okay, Dudiak, but does that mean that the truth can be anything we want it to be? Absolutely not. I am making a case for imagination as constitutive of knowledge, and of truth, but to do so responsibly I need to quickly distinguish between imagination and fantasy. In both imagination and fantasy, we are drawn to what is not, to something counter-factual, to an un-programmed future, a vision of "what might be" that is not determined by "what is." But in my admittedly idiosyncratic use of the terms, *imagination envisions that new future in response to a call that it recognizes as authoritative even while not determinative.* In imagining the counter-factual future in which the poor are liberated from systematic and inter-generational violence, we answer to the call of God, to the poor themselves, and to a healthy envisioning of the Kingdom of God on earth. *In fantasizing* about Helena Bonham Carter and the Jag and the Pacific coast highway, *I answer to no one but myself*, and that probably not in a way that is truly responsible to myself and who I am and who I am called to be, but, perhaps, as a way of avoiding who I truly am and that to which I am called. So, at least in the way that I am using the terms here, imagination is tethered to a vision of the Kingdom come, envisions a non-reality more real than actual reality, and commits itself to bringing it about, whereas fantasy is cut loose from responsibility to anything, and so has no connection to reality at all. Imagination needs to be cultivated, disciplined by a sense of vocation, free but committed; fantasy is a butterfly in swirling winds. Scientism's inability to distinguish imagination and fantasy means that, in its obsession with what is, it is blind to much of what is most real. Fantasy loses touch with "what is" and disappears into the ether; scientism gets stuck in "what is" and thus has leaden feet; but imagination opens up "what is" to ever new possibilities across obedience to the call of God.[7]

So, if in the Christian university we are to faithfully seek knowledge of the truth, we need to be at least as committed to encouraging and cultivating the imagination as we are to the discovery and the learning of facts. That is why very many Christian universities rightly insist upon a healthy dose of liberal arts courses regardless of the program in which a student is enrolled, courses which are designed precisely to spur the imagination, to provoke an ever-renewed envisioning of "what is not, but might yet be."

> "Can you see it? Can you envision the Kingdom?
> What does it look like?"

> "In the Christian university, the adventure
> begins again, anew, every autumn."

5. An invitation

In the University we are, qua university, in the knowledge business, which means that we are in the truth business. As the Christian university we need to be concerned not only with facts, but with knowledge and truth in the richer, Biblical sense that these terms bear. Because the truth in this richer sense involves not only what is the case, but what should be the case, we can, I hope, appreciate that, by this standard, true knowledge is knowledge of more than the facts, and that not all facts are "true" in this sense. This is because, on a Christian worldview, one wherein we are both interconnected with and responsible for all of creation, our faithfulness to everyone and everything, and our faithfulness to God for everyone and everything, is built into the very structure of what is most

---

7. At the same time, I would not, in the end, want to be too hard on fantasy, because curtailing fantasy in the name of imagination might well unhelpfully delimit imagination itself. That is, if imagination is to be given its fullest and necessary reign, then the line between imagination and fantasy needs to be porous—real, but not absolute.

real, and is thus a prerequisite for, rather than a diversion from, the truth. We are called, that is, to faithfully envision and make real what Jesus and his followers referred to as the Kingdom of God, or the Kingdom of Heaven. I have, that is, been arguing that the task of the Christian university is to take up in a specialized way the charge of Paul to the Corinthians to destroy arguments and every lofty opinion[8] raised "against the knowledge of God, and take every thought captive to obey Christ."[9]

Finally, I have been emphasizing the futural aspect of the Kingdom of God, that the Kingdom, which is the truth, is not a set of facts, but a call to ongoing faithfulness. That means that the Kingdom is always to come, rather than a present reality. But it also means that the Kingdom is already here insofar as we respond faithfully to God's call to neighbor love and creation care. So, while it is true that the Kingdom of God is always something we need to imagine and reimagine, it is also true that, within the Christian university, every time you forgive your roommate for drinking your last Monster Energy Drink, every time you feed an animal, every time you work hard to master the periodic table, every time you take pure joy in a novel or in a three-pointer from way downtown, every time you gather for worship or for a concert, every time you show up for class or share pizza and philosophical discussions in the dorms, insofar as you do so faithfully, you are participating in the Kingdom, making it a reality, here, now. That is, my prayer for the Christian university is not only that we come to know the truth, but that we come to experience it everyday, too.[10]

"Your Kingdom come, your will be done."[11]

"You will know the truth, and the truth will make you free."[12]

8. That is, on my reading: every knowledge not grounded in concerned, intimate familiarity.

9. 2 Cor 10:5 (NRSV).

10. Indeed, I would argue that experiencing it is a prerequisite to knowing it.

11. Matt 6:10 (NRSV).

12. John 8:32 (NRSV).

BIBLIOGRAPHY

Annie Hall. Film. UA/Jack Rollins-Charles H. Joffe, 1977.

Arendt, Hannah. *Eichmann in Jerusalem: A Report on the Banality of Evil.* New York: Penguin, 2006.

Burnyeat, Myles, M. J. Levett, and Plato. *The Theaetetus of Plato.* Indianapolis: Hackett, 1990.

CNN. Twitter Post. October 23, 2017, 6:00am. https://twitter.com/CNN/status/922402297581375488

Conway: Press Secretary Gave 'Alternative Facts'. NBCNews.com. NBC Universal News Group, 2021. https://www.nbcnews.com/meet-the-press/video/conway-press-secretary-gave-alternative-facts-860142147643.

Merica, Dan, and Sophie Tatum. "Clinton Expresses Regret for Saying 'Half' of Trump . . . - CNN." CNN Politics, September 12, 2016. https://www.cnn.com/2016/09/09/politics/hillary-clinton-donald-trump-basket-of-deplorables/index.html.

Pesic, Peter. "Proteus Rebound: Reconsidering the Torture of Nature." *Isis* 99.2 (2008) 304–17.

Roscoe, Brett. "What is Truth? A Literary Reflection." *The King's Connection* (Fall 2018) 24.

"Truthiness." https://en.wikipedia.org/wiki/Truthiness.

"Word of the Year 2016." https://en.oxforddictionaries.com/word-of-the-year/word-of-the-year-2016.

Made in the USA
Monee, IL
28 December 2022

23692315R00039